For More Information

Books

Guinness World Records, *The Best Wacky Sports World Records*. London, England: Meadowside Children's Books, 2004.

Neelman, Sol. *Weird Sports*. Heidelberg, Germany: Kehrer Verlag, 2011.

Teitelbaum, Michael. *Weird Sports.* Santa Barbara, CA: Beach Ball Books, 2011.

Websites

Topendsports
http://www.topendsports.com/sport/unusual/list.htm
A list of 100 unusual sports.

Sepak Takraw
http://www.sepaktakraw.org/about-istaf/how-to-play-the-game/#.Unjt_qX4XTQ
Full of information about how to play sepak takraw.

Publisher's note to educators and parents: Our editors have carefully reviewed these websites to ensure that they are suitable for students. Many websites change frequently, however, and we cannot guarantee that a site's future contents will continue to meet our high standards of quality and educational value. Be advised that students should be closely supervised whenever they access the Internet.

Index

B
basketball 10, 16
bossaball 28, 29
botaoshi 12, 13

C
capoeira 28
curling 14, 15
cycleball 10, 11
cycle polo 10

E
elephant polo 6, 7

H
horseball 16, 17
hugball 26, 27

K
kabaddi 18, 19

P
pato 16, 17
polo 6, 10, 11, 16

S
sepak takraw 22, 23
shrovetide football 26
soccer 10, 27, 28
street hockey 10
swamp soccer 8, 9

T
tazer soccer 27
trampolining 28

U
underwater rugby 20, 21
underwater upside-down ice hockey 4, 24
unicycle hockey 4, 5

V
volleyball 22, 23, 28

W
waterpolo 20
wrestling 18

Glossary

bogs
Wet spongy ground.

chukkas
Periods of continuous play.

contortions
Twisting out of shape.

dedicated
Specially assigned.

diameter
A line segment through the center of a circle with its ends on the circle's circumference.

disorient
To cause to be confused or lost.

gauchos
Cowboys of the South American grassy plains.

horizontally
Parallel to the horizon.

mahouts
Elephant drivers or keepers.

mallet
A club for striking a ball, as in croquet or polo.

plinth
A base often for statues.

rattan
A palm stem used especially to make furniture and wickerwork.

snorkel
A tube used by swimmers for breathing with the head underwater.

substitute
A person who takes the place of another.

textile
Cloth.

vertically
Held straight up or down from a level surface.

Bossaball is played on a specially-designed court. The court is made from inflatables with two integrated trampolines, divided across the middle by a net.

To play the game, an attacker stands on the trampoline. The rest of the team stands on the inflatable. They pass the ball to each other a maximum of five times while the attacker jumps on the trampoline to gain height. Players may only use their hands for one of the passes. The ball is then thrown to the bouncing attacker to slam the ball over the net.

WACKY FACT

"Bossa" means "style" in Portuguese. Bossa nova is a type of samba music, and music is important in bossaball. The "samba referee" usually not only makes the calls, but equipped with a microphone and percussion instruments, turns the refereeing into a DJ set!

WACKY SPORTS NEWS

Points are given for slamming the opponent's trampoline or inflatable. If the ball hits the "bossawall" around the trampoline, there is no score. More points are given for scores not using the hands. If the ball bounces on the bossawall, it is still in play. The first team to score 21 points with 2 points clear wins the set. Usually three sets are played.

Bouncing Bossaball

Bossaball is a combination of volleyball, soccer, trampolining, and elements of the Brazilian martial art capoeira. It is mainly played in Spain and Brazil, but it is also played in several other countries. It is a new sport and is getting more popular as more people see it. Bossaball was invented in Spain by Belgian Filip Eyckmans in 2004.

The bossaball court is made up of trampolines and inflatables! It is often played on the beach.

The starting plinth

The down'ards' goal

Ashbourne town's windows boarded up ready for the match.

The up'ards' goal

1 mile (1.6 km)

The goal posts are three miles apart! The entire town and river is the field. The game ends when a player bangs the ball three times on the goal wall.

WACKY SPORTS NEWS

One of the strangest soccer games ever has to be tazer soccer! It is played with a gigantic ball. All players are armed with tazers, which give small electric shocks to anyone they zap! Players can tazer anyone with the ball.

The tazer emits around 5 milliamps of electricity, which is enough to bring a person down. This game is strictly only for the crazy!

27

Mad Soccer Matches

In Ashbourne, England, shrovetide football, known as "hugball," has only one rule—no murder! The game is believed to have been played since the 12th Century. On Shrove Tuesday and Ash Wednesday at 2 p.m., a cork-filled ball is thrown from the starting **plinth** into a mob of two teams—the "up'ards" and "down'ards." There is no limit on the number of players, and anyone can take part. The game is usually played from 2 p.m. until 10 p.m. The teams form "hugs" of people moving up and down the river, trying to get the ball to their goal post.

A cork-filled ball

It's quite hard to spot the ball in the "hug"!

WACKY FACT
Tradition suggests that the "ball" was originally a severed head tossed into a waiting crowd following an execution! There is no evidence that this is true, though.

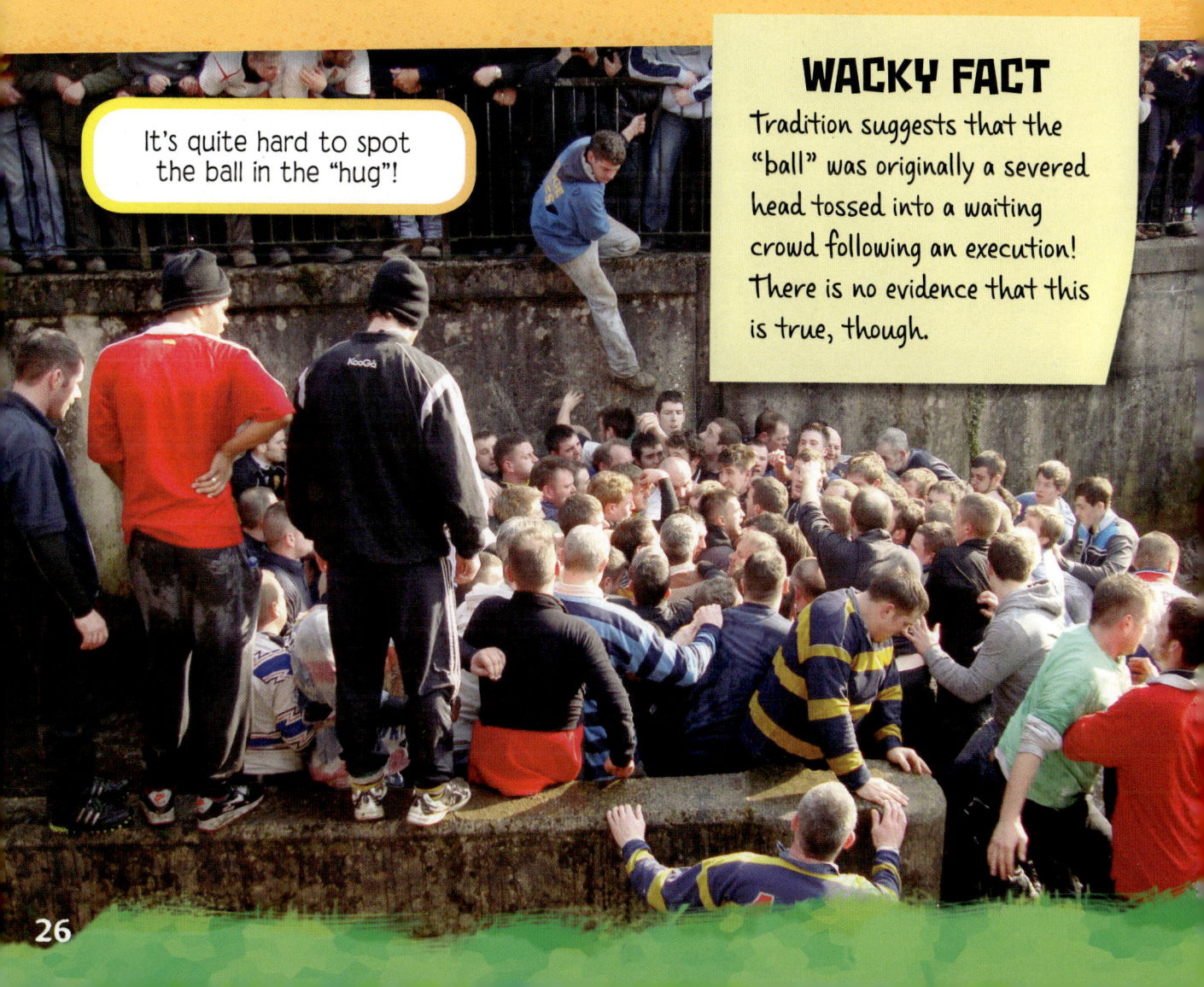

Sometimes the players pass out if they can't find the breathing hole, and underwater referees carrying oxygen tanks must dive in to save them.

WACKY FACT

Spectators must sit on the surface watching the action via a TV monitor. They occasionally see the players come up for air!

the puck

The hockey puck is made of foam so it will float.

25

Upside-Down Ice Hockey

Underwater upside-down ice hockey has to be one of the weirdest team sports ever! Players wearing wet suits play under frozen ponds or lakes by making a hole in the ice. Inside the freezing pond, they turn upside down and use the frozen ice as the playing surface! They do not use any breathing instruments. They just play until they can't hold their breath anymore.

Each team has two players. The game is played one-on-one in 10-minute intervals, with breaks every 30 seconds to allow the players to swim up so they can breathe—if they can find the hole! Holding their breath and trying to play hockey upside down can **disorient** the players, who can lose track of where the air hole is.

A hole cut in the ice for the players to enter the "pitch."

WACKY SPORTS NEWS

The first underwater upside-down ice hockey world cup was held at a lake at Weissensee, southern Austria, in February 2007 under 1 foot (30 cm) of ice in 35.6° F (2°C) water. Finland finished first, followed by Austria and Slovakia. The Czech Republic, Germany, the Netherlands, Poland, and Slovenia took part.

Weissensee, Austria

Slamming, or "spiking," the ball is much more difficult in sepak takraw than it is in volleyball. A player has to get his feet above the net to be able to slam the ball down. The player jumps and flips in the air to kick the ball. Professional sepak takraw players are athletic enough to do this and still land on their feet. A sunback or stingray spike is a scissors kick where the ball goes over the same shoulder as the kicking foot.

A sunback spike during a game of sepak takraw.

WACKY SPORTS NEWS

The sepak takraw ball is about 16 inches (40.6 cm) in diameter and usually made of **rattan** or hard plastic stems. When hit hard, the ball can travel at speeds of over 75 miles (120 km) per hour! The court and the net height and size are identical to those used in badminton.

23

Sepak Takraw

Sepak takraw is kind of like volleyball, except in sepak takraw, players cannot use their hands or arms to play. This leads to some pretty funny **contortions** to get the ball over the net! It is a very popular sport in Malaysia and Thailand. "Sepak" means "kick" in Malay, and "takraw" means "ball" in Thai.

WACKY FACT
The best sepak takraw players can kick a ball that is more than 7 feet (2.1 m) above the ground! Players have to be very agile.

The players wear fins, a diving mask, and **snorkel**. As they only use snorkels to breathe, players can only breathe when they are near the surface! Underwater rugby is one of only a few sports that can be played in 3 dimensions. Play goes on above you, below you, and to the sides, making it quite hard to keep track of where everyone is. It is also difficult to communicate with your teammates underwater, which is also a challenge!

WACKY FACT
Underwater rugby is a contact sport. A player can attack another player if they have the ball. Kicks, hits, and strangling are not allowed!

Underwater Rugby

The game of underwater rugby is played in a deep swimming pool. The teams aim to score a goal by getting a weighted ball in the opposing team's basket. During the game, six players are in the pool, while six **substitute** players wait on the side to be substituted in at any time. The ball may be passed in any direction, however, it must not leave the water.

The goals are heavy metal baskets placed at the bottom of the pool at each end. The teams start the game at each end of the pool. Each player must have one hand on the wall. The ball is in the middle of the pool, on the bottom. When the referee sounds the buzzer, both teams race to get possession of the ball.

A defender blocking the goal.

WACKY SPORTS NEWS

Underwater rugby uses a water polo ball filled with salt water rather than air. This helps the ball sink so it can be placed in the goal at the bottom of the pool.

Kabaddi can get quite rough! Here, a raider wrestles hard with a defender.

Tagged team members are "out" and temporarily sent off the field. Each time a player is out, the opposing team earns a point. A team scores a bonus of two points if the entire opposing team is out. At the end of the game, the team with the most points wins.

WACKY SPORTS NEWS

What makes this sport so unique is that the raider must hold their breath. The raider must be very skilled, very quick, and have good lungs. Try and take a breath and say "kabaddi" over and over again. How many times can you say it before you need to breathe in again? Some rulebooks say the kabaddi chant should not last longer than 30 seconds. That's a long time when you are running around not breathing!

Kabaddi, Kabaddi, Kabaddi

The skills you need to play kabaddi are wrestling, tag, and holding your breath! Two teams of seven players stand on opposite sides of a field and take turns sending a "raider" into the opponent's territory. The defenders link arms. The raider tries to tag the defenders. Meanwhile, the defenders try to stop the raider from returning back to his side before taking a breath. The raider must chant the word "kabaddi" continuously to prove that he or she is not breathing in.

WACKY FACT
Kabaddi is a very popular playground game in India, Pakistan, and Bangladesh.

defenders with linked arms

a raider

WACKY SPORTS NEWS

When the ball is dropped or falls onto the ground, anyone can pick it up so long as they are going in the same direction as the ball when it was dropped. This is to avoid any head-on-head collisions while someone is picking up the ball.

The pato net stands **vertically**, rather than **horizontally** like a basketball hoop. It is 3.3 feet (1 m) in diameter, at the top of a 7.9-foot (2.4 m) high pole. Players must make a minimum of three passes between three different players on their team before they can try to score a goal. The opposing team defends their goal by pushing their opponents using their horses' weight, or they can pull the ball from their opponent's hands.

WACKY FACT

Pato has been banned several times due to violence. Some **gauchos** have been trampled underfoot, and many more have died in knife fights during a game!

17

Pato or Horseball

Pato means "the duck game" in Spanish. Early games used to use a live duck inside a basket instead of a ball! Luckily for the ducks, that tradition has stopped now. Pato is also called horseball. It is a mixture between polo and basketball. Pato has been the national sport of Argentina since 1953. Playing fields used to stretch between neighboring ranches. The first team to reach its own ranch with the duck were the winners.

A player reaches to grab the ball by its straps in a game of pato.

The ice on the curling playing surface is slightly pebbled, not smooth and slippery like the ice on a skating rink. Curlers will often turn the stone as they throw it, helping it move across the surface. Two sweepers with brooms follow it as it slides, sweeping hard with their brooms to smooth the ice in front of the stone!

WACKY FACT

There are no judges in a curling match. Decisions are made by the captains, and scoring disputes are settled by the vice captains.

Team members quickly sweep the ice in front of the moving stone.

WACKY SPORTS NEWS

Curling was traditionally played outdoors on frozen lakes. The Grand Match (left) was an annual tournament that took place on Lake Menteith in Scotland. The match was between teams from the north and the south of Scotland. In recent years, the lake has not frozen over enough to hold the match there, so an indoor version has largely taken its place.

Bowls on Ice

Curling is a winter sport that started in Scotland. It is now an Olympic sport, but most people still think it is pretty wacky! Curling is a little like lawn bowling. Each team slides eight granite "stones" along the ice. The aim is to end up closest to the target, called the "center house."

Eight stones for each team are lined up, ready to be thrown toward the center house.

Throwers wear odd shoes. The rear shoe has a rubber sole and the front one has a slippery sole.

Two teams of four players take turns sliding the stones. The aim is to get the stone to stop in the center of the target, called the button. Curling is also called "the roaring game" because of the noise that the stone makes when it is sliding across the ice!

Attacking players only have around two and a half minutes to bring down the pole, or the defending team wins. Botaoshi may look like chaos, but each position has a special job.

WACKY FACT

Originally, the attacking team had to lower the wooden pole to a 45-degree angle, but after 1973 they had to lower the pole even further to 30 degrees.

The **defense** consists of:	The **offense** consists of:
pole supports – hold the pole upright **barriers** – protect the pole **interference** – disrupt any attack **scrum disablers** – keep the attackers from climbing on their teammates' backs **the ninja** – the man at the top of the pole, who leans his weight to keep the pole from being brought down	**scrum** – act as stepping stones so their teammates can jump toward the pole **pole attackers** – take the ninja down using their weight to topple the pole **general support attacks** – do anything to make it hard on the defense

ninja

barrier

scrum

Botaoshi Pole Battle

Botaoshi is a wacky Japanese sport where two opposing teams fight over a wooden pole. It was invented around 1955. Botaoshi is often played on sports days at schools in Japan. Cadets at Japan's Military Defense Academy in Yokosuka play a large-scale version. The two teams have 75 players each! It's quite exciting to watch the teams pulling and pushing each other.

Yokosuka, Japan

The white team is trying to defend the pole from the orange team. Teams use any means possible to try to topple the pole.

Cycleball was invented in 1893 by German laborers who wanted to play polo but couldn't afford horses. It is a popular sport in Europe and Japan. Cycleball is a mix of cycling and soccer. Players bicycle around a small court and try to smack a ball into the goal using the wheels of their bicycles or their heads. If a player puts their foot on the floor, the other team is awarded a penalty kick. There are usually just two players on each team.

Two players tussle for the ball in a cycleball match.

upright handlebars

seat over back tire

ball

WACKY SPORTS NEWS

The game used to be played with normal bikes. Nowadays, serious competitors spend a lot of money on specialty bicycles. The seats are positioned over the back tire. The bikes have a single gear. The handlebars point straight up so that the competitors can stand upright. The bikes are about twice the weight of normal bikes, too. The ball has a **textile** surface and is about 7 inches (18 cm) in diameter.

11

Bicycle Weirdness

Can you imagine playing soccer or polo on a wobbly bicycle? Cycleball and cycle polo are both pretty wacky sports. They require a lot of skill and balance.

Cycle polo is similar to polo, except bicycles are used instead of horses. The sport was invented in Ireland in 1891. It was played on a large rectangular grass field, but the faster hardcourt version pictured below is getting more popular. Called "hardcourt" or "urban" bike polo, it is played by three players on a basketball court using a street hockey ball. Cyclists have to hit the ball with their mallet. If they touch the ground with their feet they are penalized.

WACKY FACT

Cycle polo was a demonstration sport at the 1908 Summer Olympic Games! Ireland beat Germany 3-1 in the final.

WACKY SPORTS NEWS

There are about 260 swamp soccer teams around the world. There are several competitions. The World Championship is played every year on a bog in Hyrynsalmi, Finland. Around 5,000 muddy players took part in the 2005 World Championships! The European Championship is held in Ísafjörður, Iceland. The World Cup is usually held in Dunoon, Scotland. The teams think up some funny names, such as "Unathletico Mudrid" and "Mudchesthair United!"

Ísafjörður, Iceland

Hyrynsalmi, Finland

Dunoon, Scotland

Players are not allowed to change their boots during the game. Squelch!

Swamp Soccer

Swamp soccer gives a whole new meaning to the phrase "playing dirty!" Swamp soccer is played in **bogs,** or swamps. The sport is said to have come from Finland, where it was used as an exercise activity for athletes and soldiers. Playing on soft, boggy soil is very hard work.

The ball can come to a complete stop in certain parts of the field, as the ground is so wet and boggy. This means the players have to run around a lot more to reach the ball! Tactics are crucial, with a good range of body sizes and shapes needed for a team's success. In the wettest spots, the lighter players don't sink quite so badly as the heavier ones!

WACKY FACT

Swamp soccer competition organizers in Scotland recommend that players tape their footwear to their legs so that their shoes don't get lost in the swamp!

Each elephant polo match takes 14 minutes, divided into two seven-minute "**chukkas**," or halves.

WACKY FACT

At a match in 2007 in Sri Lanka, Abey, a four-ton, eighteen-year-old elephant, threw off his mahout and American rider and went on a rampage. He even destroyed the Spanish team's minibus!

Elephant Polo

Playing polo on an elephant is pretty hard. It's a long way down. Players use a standard size polo ball. The **mallet** handle needs to be between 6 and 10 feet (1.83 m and 3 m) long to reach the ground! The field is three-quarters of the length of a standard polo field, due to the slower speed of the elephants. Two people ride each elephant. The elephants are steered by **mahouts** who sit in front. The player sitting behind directs the mahout and hits the ball.

WACKY SPORTS NEWS

Elephant polo originated in Nepal. Tiger Tops, a lodge and conservation center in Nepal, is still the headquarters of elephant polo and the site of the World Elephant Polo Championships.

Tiger Tops, Nepal

WACKY SPORTS NEWS

Any stick that is legal for ice hockey, other than a goalkeeper's stick, can be used. The unicycles can have a maximum wheel **diameter** of 24 inches (61 cm). A tennis ball is typically used, although street hockey balls are also allowed.

WACKY FACT

There is no **dedicated** goalkeeper in unicycle hockey. One player usually stays back in that position to guard the goal.

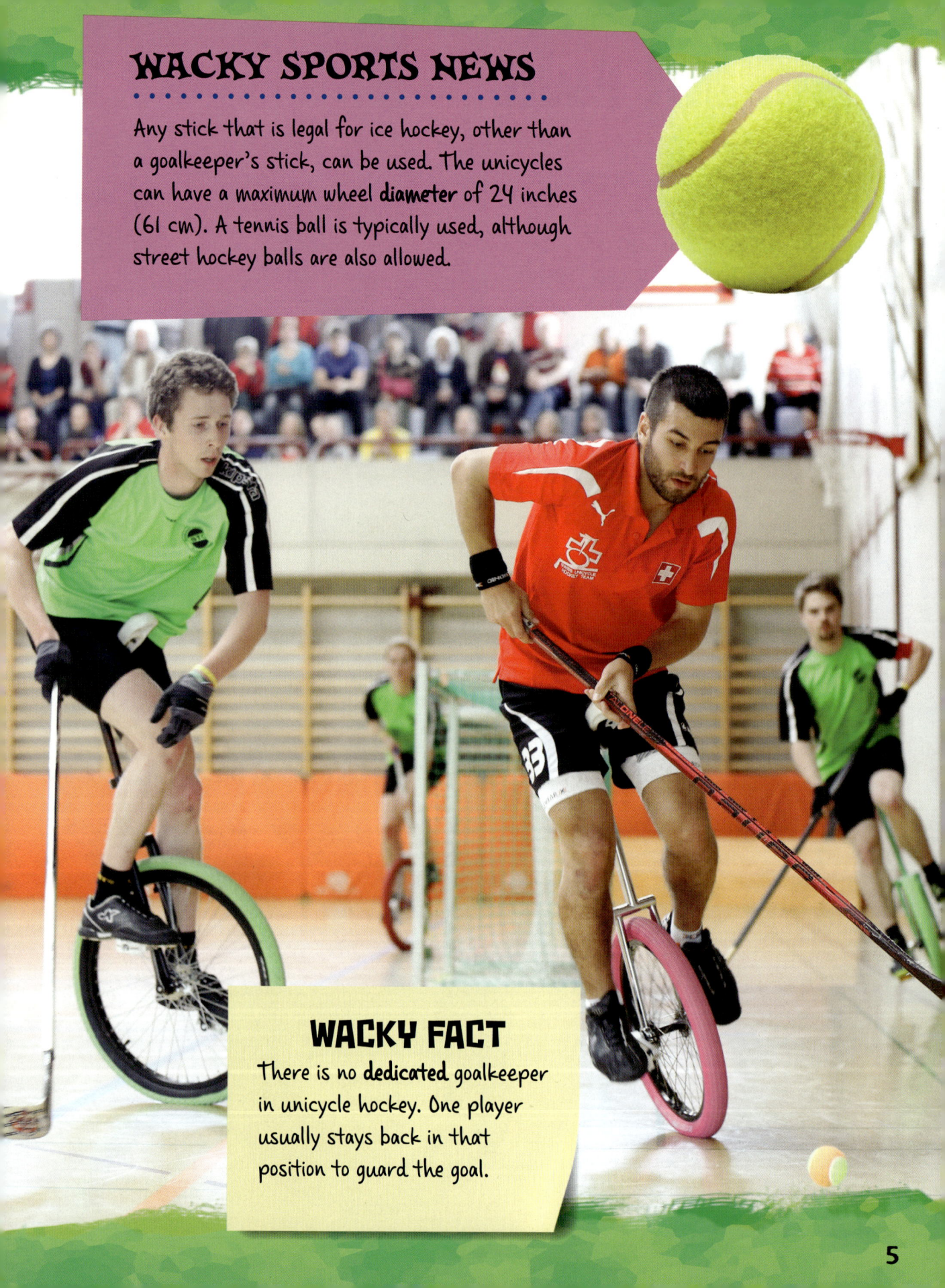

Wacky Team Sports

Teams of people get together all around the world to take part in some very weird sports. Some people decide to play ice hockey underneath a frozen lake, upside down! Other teams think playing a kind of volleyball while bouncing on trampolines and inflatable objects is a sensible way to spend the weekend. Or how about a game of hockey... on unicyles?

If you have ever tried to ride a unicycle, you know how hard it is. A unicycle is a bicycle with only one wheel. It's hard just to balance. Unicycle hockey is a fast-paced hockey game where all the players are riding unicycles. That's certainly a wacky team sport!

Unicycle hockey rules are very similar to ordinary hockey, except each player must ride a unicycle and they must keep both feet on the pedals when they play. A team is made up of five players. The court has rounded corners and barriers on all sides. The goals are set back from the end walls so that play can go behind them. Unihockey, as it is often called, is mainly played in Europe, Singapore, and Australia.

Balancing on a unicycle is not easy.

Contents

Wacky Team Sports 4
Elephant Polo 6
Swamp Soccer 8
Bicycle Weirdness 10
Botaoshi Pole Battle 12
Bowls On Ice 14
Pato or Horseball 16
Kabaddi, Kabaddi, Kabaddi 18
Underwater Rugby 20
Sepak Takraw 22
Upside-Down Ice Hockey 24
Mad Soccer Matches 26
Bouncing Bossaball 28
Glossary 30
For More Information 31
Index 32

Wacky sports can be dangerous. Do not attempt any of the sports in this book without supervision from a trained adult expert!

Please visit our website, **www.garethstevens.com**. For a free color catalog of all our high-quality books, call toll free 1-800-542-2595 or fax 1-877-542-2596.

Library of Congress Cataloging-in-Publication Data

Wood, Alix.
Wacky team sports / by Alix Wood.
p. cm. — (Wacky world of sports)
Includes index.
ISBN 978-1-4824-1224-6 (pbk.)
ISBN 978-1-4824-1243-7 (6-pack)
ISBN 978-1-4824-1499-8 (library binding)
1. Sports — Miscellanea — Juvenile literature. I. Wood, Alix. II. Title.
GV707.W66 2015
796—d23

First Edition

Published in 2015 by
Gareth Stevens Publishing
111 East 14th Street, Suite 349
New York, NY 10003

© Alix Wood Books

Produced for Gareth Stevens by Alix Wood Books
Designed by Alix Wood
Picture and content research: Kevin Wood
Editor: Eloise Macgregor

Photo credits:

Cover © 1000 Words/Shutterstock.com; 1, 9 © Guthiwoody; 4, 8, 14, 24 Shutterstock; 5 © Tscheipi; 6-7 © topten22photo/Shutterstock; 10 © Hu Totya; 11 top © Peter Huys; 11 bottom © Henry Ward; 12, 13 © Abasaa; 15 top © Herbert Kratky/Shutterstock; 15 bottom © Ewan Chesser/Shutterstock; 16, 17 bottom © Eduardo Rivero/Shutterstock; 17 top © Fioravante Patrone; 18 © Arivazhagan89; 19 top © Pal2iyawit/Shutterstock; 20 © Michael Harjes; 21 © Petter F. Schmedling; 22 © Corbis; 23 top © 3 song photography/Shutterstock; 23 bottom © Wisekwai; 25 © Alamy; 26 top © Adrian Roebuck; 26 © Mark Redfern/Paddockhousefarm.co.uk; 27 top 4 images © Adrian Roebuck; 27 bottom © iStock; 28, 29 bottom © Bossaball.net; 29 top © Pedroromero2.

All rights reserved. No part of this book may be reproduced in any form without permission from the publisher, except by reviewer.

Printed in the United States of America

CPSIA compliance information: Batch # CS15GS: For further information contact Gareth Stevens, New York, New York at 1-800-542-2595.

Wacky World of Sports

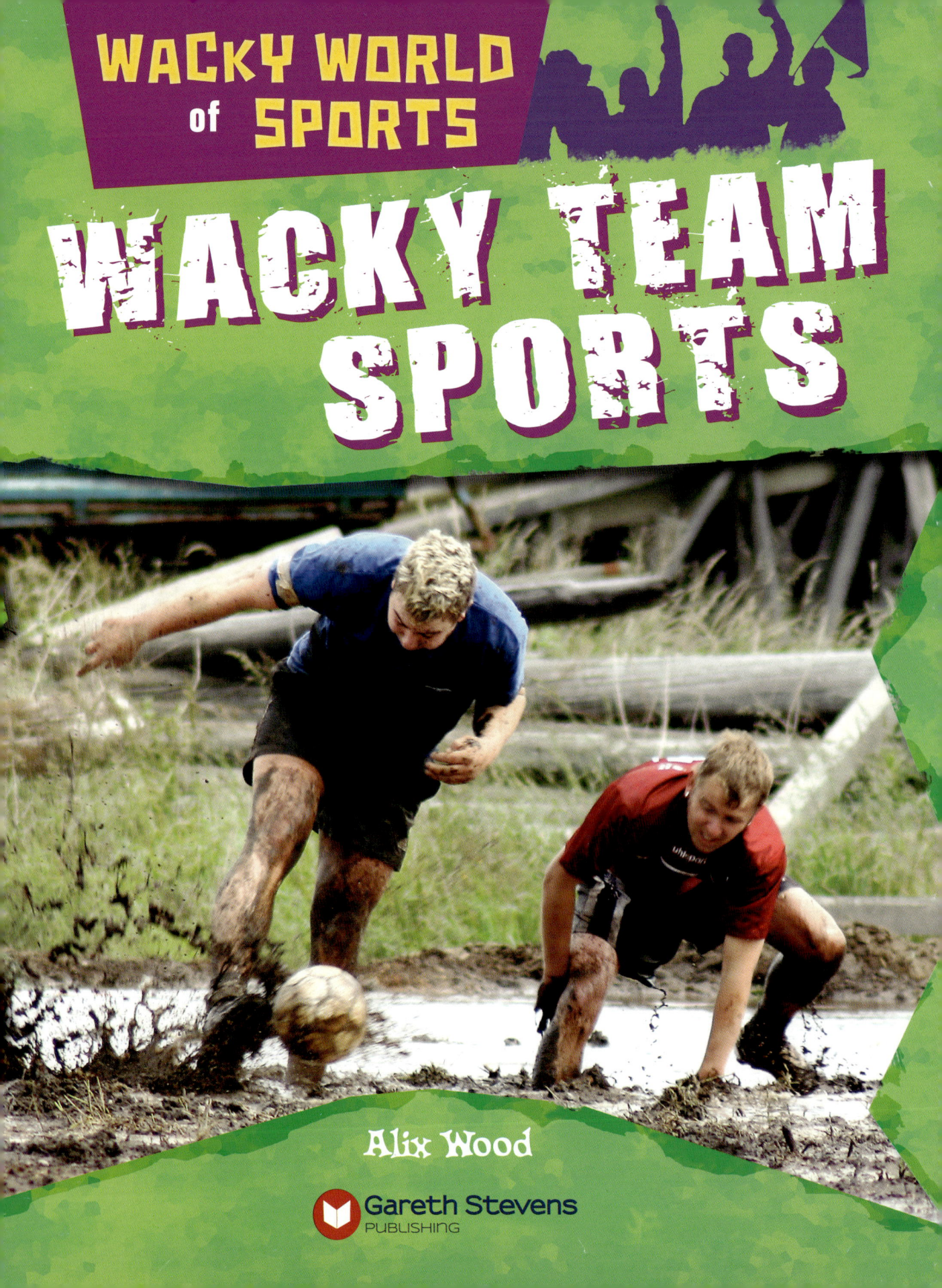

WACKY TEAM SPORTS

Alix Wood

Gareth Stevens
PUBLISHING